Self-Help Kit

Trace your Family Tree

Guidance Manual
by The Society of Genealogists

Published by
Lawpack Publishing Limited
76–89 Alscot Road
London SE1 3AW
www.lawpack.co.uk

ISBN 1 904053 11 4
All rights reserved.

Design © 2004 Lawpack Publishing
Text © 1998, 2004 Society of Genealogists

This Lawpack publication may not be reproduced in whole or in part in any form without written permission from the publisher, except that forms may be photocopied by the purchaser for his or her own use, but not for resale.

The publisher would like to thank Richard Pierce for providing family archive material for use on the cover of this Kit.

Crown copyright material is reproduced with the permission of the Controller of HMSO and the Queen's Printer for Scotland.

Exclusion of Liability and Disclaimer
Whilst every effort has been made to ensure that this Lawpack publication provides accurate and expert guidance, it is impossible to predict all the circumstances in which it may be used. Accordingly, neither the publisher, authors, retailer, nor any other suppliers shall be liable to any person or entity with respect to any loss or damage caused or alleged to be caused by the information contained in or omitted from this Lawpack publication.

Printed in Great Britain

Contents

4	Introduction
4	Beginning the search
5	Recording the information as you go
10	Developing your knowledge
11	Is somebody else working on this family?
11	Has it been done before?
13	One-name studies, family associations and clans
14	Civil registration
18	Census returns 1841–1901
20	Wills and administrations
21	Parish registers
26	Nonconformist registers
27	Society of Genealogists
31	County record offices and libraries
33	Local family history societies
34	The National Archives
36	Family History Centres
37	Some words of advice
41	Professional assistance
42	Bibliography
46	Research resources by historical period timeline
48	Index

Loose-leaf:
Ancestry Chart – 1 copy
Birth Brief – 2 copies
Family Group Sheet – 2 copies

Introduction

Welcome to the fascinating world of family history. This is an engrossing hobby which can take you in many unexpected directions and through which you will meet friendly, helpful people, whether they are researching their own family or helping others to do so.

As a family historian you will develop many skills and use a variety of sources and tools for your research. A computer is by no means necessary for family history, but there is no doubt that it can help. Not all information is on the Internet; there is still much to be found using original documents in record offices and libraries. Nevertheless the Internet is a very helpful resource, where one can discover information about records and record office, people and places. Three websites in particular will certainly help you to start:

- www.familyrecords.gov.uk – provides access to most government agencies that hold information of use to family historians with UK ancestry;
- www.a2a.pro.gov.uk – the Access to Archives consortium has lists and catalogues of many archive collections;
- www.genuki.org.uk – an incredibly useful gateway to genealogical information about the United Kingdom and Ireland.

All the web addresses included in this Manual are current as the time of going to print but web addresses are frequently changed or updated. All those included, and more, can be found at Peter Christian's website at www.spub.co.uk/tgi2/index.html.

This Manual includes information about websites, CD-ROMS, and electronic databases where relevant throughout each section, as well as introducing all the sources and record repositories that will be useful as you make your first steps in family history.

At the end of the Manual is a research strategy timeline, which will be helpful in determining what sources may be helpful for the particular period you are studying.

Also included in this Kit is a free Evaluation Version of 'Family Historian' the UK's leading genealogy software product. It allows you to store and manage a restricted amount of family history data. Its many features include creating diagrams and charts and linking images and multimedia. An introductory guide to the Evaluation Version can be found under the 'Help' menu on the main screen.

Beginning the search

Searching for your ancestors must begin with what you know about yourself, your parents and grandparents. This is the first rule: work from the known to the unknown.

Collect all the family documents you can and question your relatives. The older ones may know about letters, diaries, papers and dated photographs. They may be able to estimate ages and suggest locations, even if they cannot give the exact details of dates and places of births, marriages and deaths, which you will need to add in due course. If you are lucky, there may be birthday books or even a Family Bible containing vital dates. It is not only the dates and places which are important. Information about occupation and physical characteristics as well as family life and anecdotes should also be collected.

The source of every fact you are told or which you find in documents and books should be carefully noted. Sooner or later you will find that the various pieces of information you have collected might conflict with each other and you will need to be able to check back to see which source is likely to be more accurate. You will find that even a source such as a Family Bible cannot always be relied upon, with entries being added years after the event and dates of birth calculated incorrectly from estimated ages at death.

Remember that when you ask older people about the family no person will tell you everything that he or she knows at one sitting or in one letter. You may need to go back several times, to trigger reminiscences with old photographs and to discuss the finds in your continuing research, when 'new' names or details may unlock further memories. Do not neglect approaching younger children or cousins who may have nursed aged parents or grandparents and inherited their personal possessions. Remember that members of the family who do not appear helpful or interested may be glad to point out errors when you circulate a draft pedigree of what you have found. Never overlook cousins overseas who may have cherished family letters and photographs as links with 'home' long after copies in Britain have been destroyed.

Sometimes the vaguest of remarks may prove unexpectedly useful at a later stage and every comment should be noted, together with its source and the date on which the information was given. Family stories often contain only an element of truth, and everything should be approached with an open mind until clear proof is forthcoming.

Recording the information as you go

It is important when you begin not to trace too many lines of ancestry at the same time, else it is very easy to get overwhelmed in detail. Most people trace the male line because that is usually the surname they bear, but there is no reason why you should not trace your mother's family or some other line of ancestry if you wish.

It is equally important to record what you learn about each relative. Whether you use a card file system, loose-leaf folders, spreadsheets, databases or specially designed computer packages and programs for family historians, ensure you are systematic. It is easier to be organised and methodical from the beginning rather than wade through masses of information later on. When taking extracts from written sources keep the notes from each source separate and keep material on one family quite separate from that on another.

Dates should always be expressed as '11 November 1911' or '1911 November 11' and not as '11.11.11'. There is then no possibility of confusion between the day and the month, let alone of the century.

Always date every pedigree that you compile so that you can see which one contains the latest state of your knowledge. Photocopies of such charts, neatly written or typed, can be made cheaply and should be circulated to other members of the family as the search develops. If these charts are slightly reduced in the photocopying, then any background guidelines or joins in the paper will conveniently disappear.

No single layout can display all ancestors (male and female) as well as all cousins. For direct ancestry the 'birth brief' is appropriate. Descent layouts are based on the 'family tree' or 'indented narrative'; the latter provides ample scope for descriptive detail, the former displays relationships clearly and is valuable as a key to narrative accounts.

If you are not very methodical in your work, then you may find printed family group sheets and pedigree charts helpful, as provided in this Kit. These show immediately what is known about each family group, though they leave little space for recording other details and the sources used.

A birth brief is basically a page divided into columns for generations, divided successively into 2, 4, 8, etc., sections. The birth brief allows each individual direct ancestor to be numbered and identified, but does not allow for all the children of a couple to be noted. An example of a completed birth brief is shown opposite.

A family group sheet or card shows all the children of a particular couple and often relates back to a master birth brief. Whether you use a computer program or a paper system, you must organise your records as you go.

Printed forms are included in this Kit and on the free CD.

It will not be possible to put everything you discover on a pedigree chart, but you may find it helpful to summarise the main details on a 'drop-line pedigree chart' so that the relationships of the various members of the family, one to another, are clear. Such a chart should show full names and occupations, together with the dates and places of birth and/or baptism, marriage and death and/or burial.

A drop-line pedigree chart (see example overleaf), soon encounters practical difficulties of size and is best divided into sections. Any device will need adaptation to the space available. Suitable conventions are that:

1. spouses are linked by '=';
2. children are set out in age order across the page, linked by a line to the parents' marriage above and illegitimacy is shown by wavy lines;
3. at the least, the dates of birth and death are given below each name and of marriage after 'm' below the bride (or below the '=');
4. multiple spouses are numbered beyond the '=' so that 'man = (3)' is followed by the name of the third wife;
5. unproven descent is shown by broken lines and uncertain facts by '?';
6. descent not displayed in detail is shown by an arrow pointing down with a reference to any other chart;
7. certainty that there were no children is shown by 'no issue' below the '=';
8. to bring cousin marriages together, the age order may be distorted, but revealed by numbering in age order;
9. if crossing descent lines cannot be avoided, the vertical line is broken or looped; the example overleaf illustrates how some problems can be solved.

Birth Brief of Nova Atkinson showing parents, grandparents, great-grandparents and great-great-grandparents. Held at the Society of Genealogists and reproduced with permission of the compiler.

Trace Your Family Tree

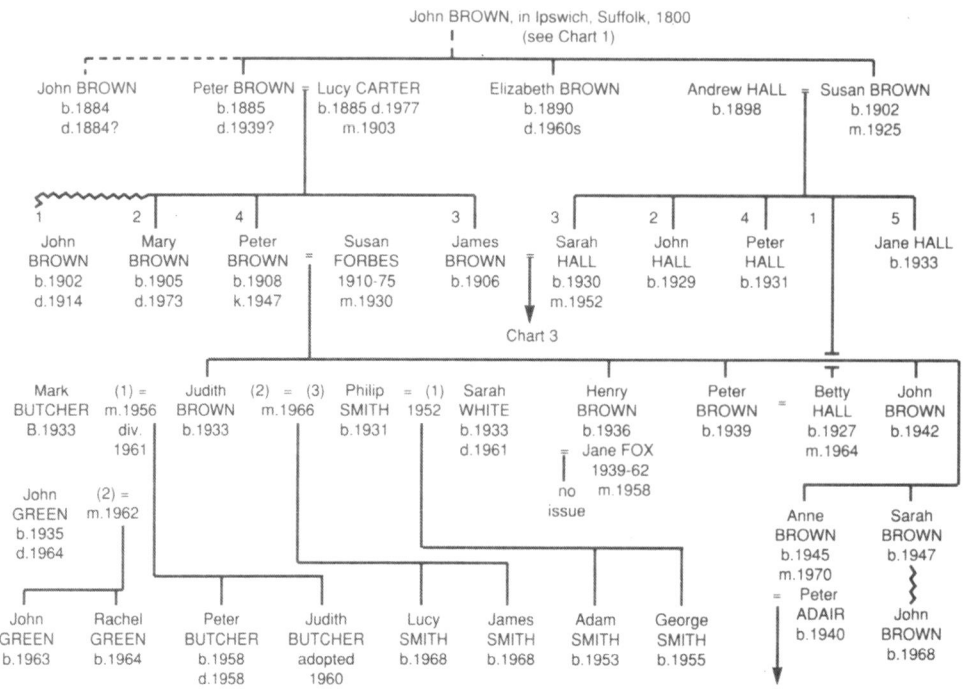

Example family tree sheet or drop-line pedigree

Completed example of the genealogical record card published by the Society of Genealogists

In whatever form the information about a family is presented, it is essential that it is clear and easy for the reader to understand. Be consistent and make a note of any abbreviations that are used, such as 'c.' for christening or 'd.' for died. Ensure that it is clear whether you are using 'b.' to mean birth or burial. A common list of abbreviations used by family historians appears below:

bach.	bachelor
b.	born
bap. or ba.	baptised
b.o.t.p	both of this parish
bur.	buried
by lic.	by licence
c.	about
co.	county
cod.	codicil
d.	died
dau.	daughter
d.s.p.	died childless
g.f.	grandfather
g.m.	grandmother
g.g.f.	great-grandfather
g.g.m.	great-grandmother
inf.	infant
lic.	licence
m. or mar.	married
MI	monumental inscription
ML	marriage licence
o.s.p or ob.s.p	died childless
o.t.p.	of this parish
pr.	(Will) proved
s.	son
spin.	spinster
unm.	unmarried
w.	wife
wdr.	widower
wid.	widow

There are several family history computer programs available that allow you to enter the information about each person as you collect it. These programs will then automatically construct pedigree charts in a variety of formats and also produce family group sheets. It is an easy matter to add a new family member or amend the details of those already included, and then produce a revised pedigree chart. Most of the better programs are described as 'Gedcom' compatible, meaning that they can receive genealogy files from other Gedcom compatible programs, and it is important that you should use one of these so that you can share your information with other researchers, and they with you.

If you begin to find a lot of information about each person then it is important to start writing a narrative account of the family as soon as possible. If you leave this until your searches are completed, it may never be done! The account, which should include your own personal reminiscences about yourself and other members of your family, can be illustrated with copies of photographs and postcard views of ancestral places. It then begins to form a permanent and valuable record for the family which is easily understood and appreciated by all its members. Several firms which specialise in copying photographs and which sell postcard views advertise in the various monthly publications. *Family Tree Magazine* and *Practical Family History* are available from major newsagents or from ABM Publishing Ltd., 61 Great Whyte, Ramsey, Huntingdon, Cambridgeshire PE17 1HL (Tel. 01487 814 050). Other leading genealogical magazines are *Family History Monthly*, Diamond Publishing Group Ltd., Unit 101, 140 Wales Farm Road, London W3 6UG, (Tel. 020 8752 8157) and *Your Family Tree Magazine*, Future Publishing Ltd., Beauford Court, 30 Monmouth Street, Bath BA1 2BW (Tel. 01225 442 244). The National Archives publishes *Ancestors*, PO Box 38, Richmond, Surrey TW9 4AJ. These national magazines provide a forum for genealogists to speak to each other and produce excellent articles on sources and techniques for family history.

Developing your knowledge

The further back you get, the more scanty family information will become in most if not all lines. Therefore, while you are visiting older members of the family it will be necessary for you to read about the next steps.

Of the many books of advice, the following can be recommended: *Tracing your Family Tree*, J. Cole & J. Titford, (Countryside Books, Newbury, 1997); *Ancestral Trails: The Complete Guide to British Genealogy and Family History*, M.D. Herber (Sutton Publishing, Stroud, 2nd edn. 2004); and *Explore your Family's Past* (Reader's Digest Association, 2000).

For those with Irish, Scottish and Welsh ancestry the following books can be recommended: *Tracing your Irish Ancestors: The Complete Guide*, J. Grenham (Gill and Macmillan, Dublin, 1999); *Tracing your Scottish Ancestry*, K.B. Cory (Polygon, Edinburgh, 2nd edn. 1997); and *Welsh Family History: A Guide to Research*, J. Rowlands et al (Federation of Family History Societies, 2nd edn. 1998).

If you find reference to some source of information which you do not fully understand, then *The Dictionary of Genealogy*, T. FitzHugh (A. & C. Black, London, 5th edn 1998) or *The Family Historian's Enquire Within*, P. Saul (Federation of Family History Societies, 5th edn. with amendments 1997) may be helpful. Useful explanations can be found in *Oxford Companion to Local and Family History*, D. Hey (Oxford University Press, 1996).

Is somebody else working on this family?

As there are many thousands of people throughout the world who are tracing their ancestors it is as well to see if there is anyone else working on the same line as yourself. An enormous number of families in which people are interested have been listed in various commercial directories and these should not on any account be overlooked. Check as many as you can; duplication of effort is wasteful, but sharing research with relatives can be of great benefit to both parties.

Many people advertised the surnames on which they were working in the *National Genealogical Directory* which was published annually between 1979 and 1993 (originally by M.J. Burchall and latterly by I. Caley). Many more entries appear in the *Genealogical Research Directory* (ed. by K.A. Johnson & M.R. Sainty, Library of Australian History, Sydney) that has been published annually since 1981 and is widely available. Each issue contains at least a 100,000 entries. Those who advertise their interests in one issue, however, may not do so in the next and it is worthwhile to check as many editions as possible. The *Genealogical Research Directory*, which relates to families being researched all over the world, also contains the addresses and other details of most family history societies worldwide.

Many local family history societies (see 'Local family history societies' below) have published lists of their members' 'interests' and other searchers publish their interests in the monthly magazines mentioned above. The Society of Genealogists (see 'Society of Genealogists' below) maintains an index of its own 'Members' Interests'. The largest single index of this kind is the *British Isles Genealogical Register* (known as 'BIG-R') which lists families being researched in the United Kingdom only. Three editions have been published since 1994 on microfiche or now on CD-ROM. The latest BIG–R 2000, lists 374,000 entries relating to 155,000 surnames.

The World Wide Web allows access to millions of researchers by using the various local area interest lists maintained by volunteers or on www.rootsweb.com. Many British researchers' surnames lists can be found by accessing www.genuki.org.uk. The Church of Latter Day Saints publishes its Pedigree Resource files on www.familysearch.org. Some commercial sites such as www.genesconnected.com allow you to enter your research data in the hope that others are researching the same names and charge a small fee if you want to contact a researcher. See *The Genealogist's Internet*, P. Christian (The National Archives, 2nd edn. 2003) and *The Good Web Guide: Genealogy* (The Good Web Guide Ltd., 3rd edn, 2003).

Has it been done before?

If a family history has already been researched and published in book form you will find a reference to it in *Catalogue of British Family Histories*, T.R. Thomson (3rd edn. London, 1980).

Accounts of families are to be found in many local and county histories, biographical studies, national and local periodicals, transactions of archaeological and record societies and in a multitude of out-of-the-way and forgotten books. In the last century, Dr. G.W. Marshall went through works of this nature making notes of every tabular pedigree or account of a family that he came across which gave at least three generations in the male line. These are all listed in his *The Genealogist's Guide* (4th edn. 1903; reprinted London & Baltimore, 1967).

Marshall's Guide will give you references to most pedigrees printed before 1903, but some of those he missed and most of those published in the first 50 years of the last century were indexed by Major J.B. Whitmore in *A Genealogical Guide* (London 1953).

Continuing Whitmore's work, G.B. Barrow published another volume also called *The Genealogist's Guide* (London & Chicago, 1977) listing family history material which was published in the next 25 years.

Together these three books – and you must consult all three – list most material printed on any family in England, and they are quite indispensable. If you want to come a little more up to date, you will find in the back of Thomson's *Catalogue*, mentioned above, an Appendix of family histories printed between 1975 and 1980 which is the only compilation of its kind for this period.

These authors made no particular search for Scottish and Irish material. For printed pedigrees of Scottish families you will need to consult *Scottish Family History*, M. Stuart (Edinburgh, 1930), which was brought up to date by *Scottish Family Histories*, J.P.S. Ferguson (Edinburgh, 2nd edn. 1986). The latter lists in addition those Scottish libraries known to possess copies. Both should be consulted.

For Irish printed pedigrees there are two books: *Bibliography of Irish Family History and Genealogy*, B. de Breffny (Cork, 1974) and the more up-to-date *Bibliography of Irish Family History*, E. MacLysaght (Dublin, 1982). Both should be consulted.

Your public library will probably not have all the books and periodicals mentioned in these bibliographies and it may not be easy to find copies of particular items. Many will be found at the Society of Genealogists (see 'Society of Genealogists' below). If you go to the Society for the bibliographies you will find them on the Textbook Shelves in the Middle Library and on all other floors.

If there is nothing in print, the Society may have a typescript or manuscript family history. You will need to consult the Library Catalogue; that will tell you if there is any bound material. Unbound manuscript research notes are kept in the Document Collection in the Lower Library where there are files on many thousands of families in alphabetical order. Material received since 1992 has been microfiched and the fiche are available in the Lower Library. After that, you should look at the card index of pedigrees in deposited and other special collections.

The Society of Genealogists is always glad to add any pedigree to its collection and its receipt will automatically be mentioned in the *Genealogists' Magazine*. If your donation includes your address, this is an effective method of getting in touch with other people interested in the same surname, both now and in the future.

If the family has a hereditary right to a coat of arms you may find that a pedigree has been registered at the College of Arms, Queen Victoria Street, London EC4V 4BT (Tel. 020 7248 2762, www.college-of-arms.gov.uk). No list of the pedigrees registered there has been printed. However, a pedigree may have been registered at the College at the time of a grant of arms and an index of many grants of arms before 1898 is to be found in *Grantees of Arms Before 1898* (Harleian Society, Vols. 66–68, London, 1915–17).

A pedigree may also have been given to the local family history society of the area to which it relates (see 'Local family history societies' below) or to the appropriate county record office (see 'County record offices and libraries' below).

As mentioned above, many family history societies have published lists of the families on which their members are working, and articles about their research may also appear in their magazines. A card index of articles on families and other matters which have appeared in local family history society magazines since 1976 is maintained at the Society of Genealogists.

As your search develops, and you go further back in time finding perhaps that your ancestors have moved from one county to another, you will need to consult these various indexes again. References which seem irrelevant when you commenced your work may later suddenly acquire greater relevance.

Remember, however, that a published or manuscript pedigree is not necessarily either complete or accurate. Its accuracy can only be judged by the extent to which it quotes the authorities on which it has been based. You may, therefore, need to check it carefully against parish registers, Wills and other original documents.

Another warning needs repeating here. Because a family of the same surname has been traced in the past, even in the same locality, that does not mean that there is necessarily a relationship. Concentrate on your own immediate family and work steadily back on that; resist all temptation to work down from some presumed ancestor with the same surname. That is a sure way of tracing other people's ancestors.

One-named studies, family associations and clans

Some genealogists trace everyone with a particular surname and, if they are willing to share and exchange information about it, they may belong to the Guild of One-Name Studies or 'GOONS' (Box G, 14 Charterhouse Buildings, Goswell Road, London EC1M 7BA). The Guild has about 1,800 members researching over 5,000 surnames plus variant spellings. A list of the families on which they are working is given in the Guild's *Register of One-Name Studies*, which is published annually (GOONS, 14th edn. 2000). The register is updated regularly on the Guild's excellent website www.one-name.org and further information can be obtained from the Guild's quarterly journal. Other 'one-name' searchers are listed in the *Genealogical Research Directory* and in the *British Isles Genealogical Register*.

There are also many family associations worldwide. Those which published some kind of periodical or newsletter are listed in *Surname Periodicals: A World-Wide Listing of One-Name Genealogical Publications*, I.J. Marker and K.E. Warth (GOONS, 1987). Others appear in *Directory of Family Associations*, E.P. Bentley (Baltimore, USA, 3rd edn. 1996).

A list of the Chiefs of Clans and Names in Scotland, with their addresses, is published annually in *Whitaker's Almanack*, J. Whitaker (A. & C. Black, London) and a list of the family surname organisations which have been dubbed 'Clans of Ireland' can be obtained from the Clans of Ireland Office, Grange Clare, Kilmeague, Naas, Co. Kildare, Republic of Ireland.

With all this activity you may think that there is little left to be done, but the great majority of people tracing their ancestors find that the work they are doing, at least in the early stages, is unique and has not been done before. After that there is quite likely to be an overlap with someone somewhere. If you deposit copies of the fruits of your labours at the Society of Genealogists as soon as you can, you are likely to make contacts and discover long-lost cousins much sooner than you think.

Civil registration

From the above mentioned you will learn that for births, marriages and deaths in England and Wales since 1 July 1837, details of names, dates, ages, addresses and occupations can be obtained by purchasing certificates at the Family Records Centre, 1 Myddelton Street, London EC1R 1UW (Tel. 0870 243 7788, open Monday, Wednesday & Friday 9.00–5.00; Tuesday 10.00–7.00, Thursday 9.00–7.00 and Saturday 9.30–5.00). (First-time visitors to the Centre may wish to prepare themselves by reading *The Family Record Centre: A User's Guide*, S. Colwell (National Archives, 2002).

Here, on the ground floor and in a section of the building run by the General Register Office, you may search the quarterly indexes of births, marriages and deaths without charge. There are four indexes per year noting the events recorded between January and March (March quarter); April to June (June quarter); July to September (September quarter) and October to December (December quarter). Before 1911 these merely show the name of the person registered and the place of registration, though the deaths indexes include the stated age at death from 1866 onwards. Their value, however, lies in the fact that they cover all England and Wales in one alphabetical series.

The full biographical detail and connecting information is only available if you purchase a certificate. Each certificate costs £7 (at the time of writing) and takes four days to prepare. You may wish to collect it and then carry out the next stage of the search, or you can have it posted without further charge. If there is more than one likely entry in the indexes for the event you require you may ask for each to be checked against a known fact (e.g. the exact date of birth or the name of the father). If an entry does not agree with the facts you have given, then £4 is returned to you.

About 2,000 people a day use these indexes and it is advisable to avoid the crush in the search room, particularly at lunchtime, by going on a Monday or Friday or for the first hour in the morning. Overcoats and bags should be left in the lockers in the basement (operated by a £1 coin which is refunded) and bored family members may stay in the refreshment room there. If you cannot go yourself, you will find advertisements of many searchers who offer special rates for work there in the various monthly genealogical magazines (details are at the end of 'Recording the information as you go' above).

A marriage certificate from 1914; unusually the groom has changed his name.

The usual manner of working is to search for a known birth, such as that of your father or grandfather, and then with the information on that birth certificate to search for the marriage of his parents, working backwards from the date of birth until the marriage is found (each party having the same reference in the indexes). The marriage certificate will normally give an indication of the age of the parties so that their births can be searched for and the process repeated.

Of course one's exact age at any time was less important in the past than it is now. Ages on death certificates are frequently incorrect and those on marriage certificates should always be treated with caution. They may have been raised or lowered for a variety of reasons.

Copies of the indexes are available in some libraries on microfilm or microfiche and there is a set at the Society of Genealogists from 1837 to 1926. Certificates may be obtained by post, fax or email from the General Register Office, PO Box 2, Southport, PR8 2JD (Tel. 0870 243 7788; www.gro.gov.uk/gro/content), but cost £11.50, to include a three-year search, unless the exact reference from the indexes is known, when the charge is (currently) £8.50 or £7 if ordered online. UK residents can order certificates online by visiting www.col.statistics.gov.uk. Alternatively, if you know the district the event occurred in, you can buy certificates from the relevant register office.

Images of the indexes from 1837–2001 are available on a commercial website www.1837online.com which allows the indexes to be viewed and searched for a modest fee. FreeBMD (http://freebmd.rootsweb.com) is a collaborative project to transcribe the civil registration indexes of births, marriages and deaths for England and Wales from 1837 and to provide free Internet access to the transcribed entries. The database is not yet complete; as of October 2003 it contained over 68 million records.

A birth or death taking place at the end of one quarter may be registered and appear in the indexes for the next quarter. Registration of births was far from complete in the early years of civil registration and occasionally the indexes themselves are incomplete. If you are unable to locate an event, an approach should be made to the local Registrar of Births and he or she may then be able to identify the entry. An unregistered child may in any case have been baptised and appear in the appropriate church registers. A very large number of baptisms between 1837 and 1875 are to be found on the International Genealogical Index (see 'Parish registers' below). It was quite easy to give an illegitimate child the appearance of a legitimate birth certificate and if the marriage of the parents of a child cannot be found then it is useful to assume that one of the parents is already married to someone else and to search for that marriage.

Other reasons for the apparent non-registration of a birth or marriage are that variations in the forenames and even the surname itself have not been taken into account. Many people in the last century assumed additional forenames at marriage or in later life. Many others prior to the introduction of basic elementary education in the 1870s had no conception of a 'correct' spelling for their surname and the sound which they made when repeating it might well be transmitted to paper in different ways by different people. This is an important point to bear in mind the further back you go, and you should always be on the look-out for possible variations in the surname you are researching.

Events in Scotland

For such events in Scotland from 1855, apply to the Search Unit, New Register House, 3 West Register Street, Edinburgh EH1 3YT (Tel. 0131 314 4433; open Monday to Thursday 9.00–4.30, Friday 9.00–4.00). The General Register Office for Scotland now provides access to birth marriage and death records through the website www.scotlandspeople.gov.uk. There is a free surname search where you can see how many entries there are under your name on the indexes. You can pay to search for and download indexed digital images of the statutory registers of births 1855–1902, deaths 1855–1952 and marriages 1855–1927.

Computerised indexes from 1855 to date may be consulted for a half-hourly charge of £4 on the ground floor of the Family Records Centre, London, as part of 'Scotlink'. Advance booking is possible but not essential. The indexes are also available on microfilm, 1855–1920 only, at the Society of Genealogists.

Events in Ireland

The address for Northern Ireland events from 1922 is the General Register Office (Northern Ireland), Oxford House, 49–55 Chichester Street, Belfast BT1 4HL (Tel. 028 9025 2000; www.groni.gov.uk). Earlier certificates and those for the rest of Ireland from 1864 (with non-Catholic marriages from 1845) can be obtained from the General Register Office, Joyce House, 8–11 Lombard Street East, Dublin 2 (Tel. 00 353 1 635 4000; www.groireland.ie). The GRO Northern Ireland has a computerised index of births and deaths from 1864. The facility can be booked at the office for £8 for six hours which includes verification of up to four entries by staff with an option of further verifications at £1.50 each.

Events overseas and in the Army

Also at the Family Records Centre, 1 Myddelton Street, London EC1R 1UW are various indexes to events overseas and in the army. The chief ones are:

- Consular Returns: births, marriages and deaths of British subjects overseas 1849–1965.
- Marine Register: births and deaths at sea 1837–1965.
- Regimental Returns: births in the United Kingdom and overseas 1761–1924. The overseas returns start in about 1790.
- Army Chaplains' Returns: overseas births, marriages and deaths 1796–1965.
- War Deaths: Natal and South Africa Forces 1899–1902, First World War 1914–1921, Second World War 1939–1948.

Because many of these overseas and army records duplicate and overlap with records held elsewhere (in the National Archives and the Guildhall Library) it is wise to read the section on 'Births, Marriages and Deaths of Britons Overseas' in *Tracing your Ancestors in the Public Record Office*, A. Bevan (National Archives, 6th edn. 2002) before purchasing certificates. This supplements the valuable country by country survey in *The British Overseas: A Guide to Records of their Births, Baptisms, Marriages,*

Deaths and Burials, Available in the United Kingdom, G. Yeo (Guildhall Library, 3rd revised edn. 1994), but its general introductory pages must also be consulted. Also useful is *Tracing Births, Deaths and Marriages at Sea*, C.T. & M.J. Watts (Society of Genealogists, 2004).

Events in India

Perhaps one should add here that the records of births, marriages and deaths in India (including Burma and Aden), with indexes, from 1698 to 1948, originally returned to the East India Company, are now at the Oriental & India Office Collections, British Library, Asia Pacific & Africa Collections, 96 Euston Road, London NW1 2DB (Tel. 020 7412 7873; www.bl.uk/collections/orientaloffice.html; Email: oioc-enquiries@bl.uk).

Census returns 1841–1901

Once you know where some of your relatives were living a hundred or more years ago, you can consult the official census returns for 1901, 1891, 1881, 1871, 1861 and 1851, which record street by street the members of each household, their relationship to its head, ages, occupations and birthplaces. The first census of 1841 is also available, but it does not show relationships or precise places of birth.

A complete set of the census returns for England, Wales, the Isle of Man and the Channel Islands can be seen without charge on microfilm, microfiche (or on the Internet for 1901) on the first floor at the Family Records Centre (see 'Civil registration' above), in a section of the building run by the National Archives. No reader's ticket is needed to consult the census returns. Here there are street indexes for the larger towns and a good collection of surname indexes. First-time visitors may care to read *Making Use of the Census*, S. Lumas (National Archives, 2002), which explains the procedures in a helpful way.

Microfilms of census returns for particular counties are often held by county record offices (see 'Country record offices and libraries' below) and city libraries and many have been indexed by surname by local family history societies. For the available indexes see *Marriage and Census Indexes for Family Historians*, J. Gibson & E. Hampson (Federation of Family History Societies, 8th edn. 2000). The National Archives has licensed images of the census returns to be sold on CD-ROM by a number of companies including S. &. N British Data Archives Ltd. (www.britishdataarchive.com).

Name indexes to the three most recent censuses available to family historians can be accessed via the Internet. The National Archives has indexed the 1901 census and the images of the returns for England and Wales can be viewed online for a modest fee on www.1901census.nationalarchives.gov.uk. 'Ancestry' at www.ancestry.co.uk is a subscription site that includes an index and images of the 1891 census for England and Wales. This site can be viewed free of charge at the Society of Genealogists. A transcription and index to the 1881 census are freely available on www.familysearch.org. CD-ROM versions of the 1881 index can be purchased from the Genealogical Society of Utah to use at home.

Extract of the 1901 census for Dukestown in Tredegar, Monmouthshire, from the National Archives website.

Large collections of census indexes for other years are also to be found at the Society of Genealogists (see 'Society of Genealogists' below) and the Family Record Centre (see 'Civil registration' above).

People do not always know or tell the truth about their ages and places of birth and it is wise to search all the available census returns for possible variant information as well as for additional members of the family. The ages and places of birth of the parents of a child born in 1890 may, for instance, be found from the 1891 census returns and then similar details of the grandparents found from the 1871 returns of these places of birth (or perhaps more easily from the indexed 1881 returns), with perhaps the great-grandparents being found in the same way in 1851. Even the ages and places of birth of the parents of a person who was born about 1815 and who married in 1840 may still be discovered from the 1851 returns if they survived to that date.

The Scottish census returns 1841–1901, arranged by parish are available at New Register House, 3 West Register Street, Edinburgh EH1 3YT, where a fee is charged. Indexes and images of the 1881–1901 Scottish censuses can be found on www.scotlandspeople.gov.uk. Many returns and indexes for other years are held in the Library of the Society of Genealogists.

The first complete Irish census that survives is that for 1901, which, with that for 1911, can be seen at the National Archives of Ireland, Bishop Street, Dublin 8, Eire; they are arranged by town and or, in urban areas, by street.

Wills and administrations

Much useful information can be gleaned from Wills and administrations, copies of which for England and Wales going back to 1858 may be seen and photocopies obtained (£5 each) at the Principal Registry of the Family Division, First Avenue House, 42–49 High Holborn, London WC1V 6NP (Tel. 020 7947 6000; open Monday to Friday, 10.00–4.30). No reader's ticket or appointment is required. Documents can take an hour to be produced but it is more usual to arrange to collect them or have them posted on.

For those with something to bequeath, the annual Will indexes on the open shelves here are more informative than death certificates. They show date and place of death as well as the names (and, in early years, relationships) of a testator's executors. 'Letters of administration' are granted when someone dies without leaving a Will. From 1858 to 1870 the Wills and administrations are indexed separately but from 1871 onwards they are indexed together in annual volumes covering all of England and Wales. Wills of people who died overseas but with property in England or Wales also appear.

The indexes are easier and quicker to use than the General Register Office death indexes at the Family Records Centre and if you are searching over a long period or cannot find the death entries you require, a search here is recommended. In cases where the surname is very frequent the Will indexes may be used to eliminate possible entries found in the death indexes.

There are copies of the indexes of Wills and administrations in some major libraries and District Probate Registries. There is a set on microfiche 1858–1943 at the Family Records Centre (see 'Civil registration' above) and there are microfilm copies 1858–1930, re-organised by the initial letter of the surname, at the Society of Genealogists (see 'Society of Genealogists' below). Postal searches can be undertaken by the York Postal Searches & Copies Department, The Probate Registry, Duncomb Place, York YO1 7EF (Tel. 01904 624 210). The fee of £5 includes a copy of the Will and a four-year search. Additional four-year searches of the indexes cost £3.

Prior to 1858 a Will was 'proved' in one of the 300 local church courts depending on where the deceased's personal property was located. The Family Records Centre (see 'Civil registration' above) holds records 1383–1858 of the Prerogative Court of Canterbury, the senior probate court in England and Wales, with many Wills for London, the south-east of England and some for those who died overseas and had property in the United Kingdom. Fully alphabetical indexes are available there for the period 1383–1800 and 1853–1858, otherwise the manuscript calendars must be searched. All the Wills are indexed and available online through the National Archives documents online service at www.nationalarchives.gov.uk. Copies of the Wills can be downloaded at £3 each.

The Family Record Centre also holds copies of the Estate Duty Office Registers 1796–1858 that contain abstracts (i.e.summaries) of most Wills in England and Wales 1815–1858.

Wills proved in the subsidiary church courts before 1858 are usually to be found in the appropriate county record offices (see 'County record offices and libraries' below). If the Will was proved between 1796 and 1858, then you may be able to discover in which ecclesiastical court by looking at the indexes to the Estate Duty Registers. The Society of Genealogists (see 'Society of Genealogists' below) holds copies of indexes for many of them.

Parish registers

Before Civil Registration started (1837 in England and Wales, 1855 in Scotland and 1864 in Ireland) births and deaths were not recorded as such, rather baptisms, marriages and burials were entered in the registers of the appropriate churches or chapels.

Some parish – Church of England – registers date from 1538. Most of those over 100 years old are now deposited in county record offices and very few remain in parish churches. Access to original registers in public hands is mostly free; for those at the church the clergy are allowed to make a charge (from 1 January 2003: £15 for the first hour and £12 for each subsequent hour or part of an hour).

The whereabouts of any register may be determined from *The Phillimore Atlas and Index of Parish Registers*, C.R. Humphery-Smith (Phillimore, 3rd edn. 2002) and the addresses and opening hours of the record offices mentioned are shown in *Record Repositories in Great Britain* (Historical Manuscripts Commission, 11th edn. 1999). Most record offices have a website which lists the registers that they hold. Details can be found via

Trace Your Family Tree

[Page 1st]

BAPTISMS solemnized in the Parish of *Spilsby* in the County of *Lincoln* in the Year 1813

When Baptized	Child's Christian Name	Parent's Name (Christian)	Parent's Name (Surname)	Abode	Quality, Trade, or Profession	By whom the Ceremony was Performed
1813 Jan. 10 No. 1	Thomas Bastard Son of	Dymoke & Liddy	Ward Day	Spilsby Spilsby	Joiner Whore	Revd. Trollope Off. Min.
Jan 10 No. 2	Lucy Bastard Daughtr. of	John & Liddy	Goodrick Day	Keal Coats Spilsby	Publican Whore	Revd. Trollope Off. Min.
Jan 12 No. 3	William Son of	Jonathan & Jane	Shephard	Spilsby	Joiner	Revd. Wm. Emlyn Off. Min.
Jan 13 No. 4	Maria Daughter of	Thomas & Mary	Ashton Wynne	Spilsby Spilsby	Labourer Strumpet	Revd. Wm. Brackenbury Off. Min.
Feb 24 No. 5	Thomas Son of	John & Mary	Bailey	Spilsby	Cordwainer	Revd. Wm. Brackenbury Off. Min.
Feb 28 No. 6	Francis Richd. Son of	Richd. & Martha	Cross	Spilsby	Blacksmith	Revd. Trollope Off. Min.
March 7th No. 7	William Son of	Philip & Mary	Thompson	Spilsby	Publican	Revd. Trollope Off. Min.
March 14 No. 8	Harby Son of	Harby & Mary	Hill	Spilsby	Farmer	Revd. Wm. Brackenbury Off. Min.

The first page from the 1813 Baptismal Register of Spilsby in Lincolnshire; it includes some frank descriptions made by the vicar; the original is at the Lincolnshire Record Office.

www.genuki.org.uk or via the Historical Manuscript Commission's gateway to record offices known as ARCHON at www.archon.nationalarchives.gov.uk/archon/.

Over the years a great many parish registers have been copied and indexed, often to 1812 (when the form of the baptismal and burial registers changed and printed columns were introduced) or to 1837 or later. Many more have been microfilmed by the Genealogical Society of Utah. The largest collection of these copies in the British Isles is at the Society of Genealogists. The places and years covered are given in a series of individual *County Guides* published by the Society. Details can also be found on the Society's website www.sog.org.uk. From the various available copies, three important centralised indexes have been compiled:

(1) **International Genealogical Index:** this contains about 80,000,000 baptisms and marriages from parish registers between 1538 and 1875. They are arranged in alphabetical order of surname and forename in county sections. Variations in the surnames have been brought together. The dates are those of baptisms not of birth. This index, compiled by the Genealogical Society of Utah is known as the International Genealogical Index (or IGI). Several editions have been produced on microfiche (the most recent in 1992) and it is widely available in county record offices, libraries and Family History Centres (see 'Family History Centres' below). At some centres the 1988 or 1992 edition with its addenda can be consulted on computers where it forms part of a group of programs known as *FamilySearch*. The computerised version allows country-wide searches to be made for a particular baptism or marriage, or, in a 'parent search', for the children born to a marriage. An online version can be found at www.familysearch.org. A full set includes material from every country worldwide as well as events at sea and it contains hundreds of millions of entries of baptism and marriage. An indication of the parishes and periods covered is provided by the microfiche 'Parish and vital records list', but it should be used with care. The database is an important tool but is by no means complete or totally accurate. Supplements to the British section of the IGI are published on CD-ROMs known as the *British Isles Vital Records Index*.

(2) **Boyd's Marriage Index:** this contains about 7,000,000 marriages in England between 1538 and 1837, arranged in alphabetical order of surname and forename in 25-year sections, divided by county, in 531 volumes. More than 4,000 parishes and periods covered are listed in *A List of Parishes in Boyd's Marriage Index* (Society of Genealogists, 6th edn. 1994). There is a typescript copy of the index at the Society of Genealogists and microfiche copies are available at many Family History Centres (see 'Family History Centres' below). The index can be consulted online at www.englishorigins.com.

(3) **Pallot's Marriage Index:** covers most marriages in the London area 1780–1837. Originally arranged in alphabetical order in one sequence on paper slips, postal searches are possible. Apply to Achievements Ltd., 79–82 Northgate, Canterbury, Kent CT1 1BA. Fees are payable; the minimum charge being £20. The index has been published on CD-ROM and can be accessed through an online subscription service at www.ancestry.co.uk. This can be used free of charge at the Society of Genealogists.

MARRIAGES solemnized in the Parish of *Saint Weonard's* in the County of *Hereford* in the Year 18*34*

William Webb of *the* Parish of *Ledbury in the county of Hereford, Bachelor* and *Jane Watkins* of *this* Parish *Spinster* were married in this *Church* by *Banns* ~~with Consent of~~ this *twenty-ninth* Day of *April* in the Year One thousand eight hundred and *thirty four* By me *Thomas William Webb, Curate*

This Marriage was solemnized between us { *William Webb* / The mark T of *Jane Watkins* }

In the Presence of { *William Watkins* / *Mary Taylor* }

No. 64.

Luke Powell of *this* Parish *Bachelor* and *Mary Ann Rudge* of *this* Parish *Spinster* were married in this *Church* by *Licence* ~~with Consent of~~ this *ninth* Day of *May* in the Year One thousand eight hundred and *thirty four* By me *Thomas William Webb, Curate*

This Marriage was solemnized between us { *Luke Powell* / *Mary Ann Rudge* }

In the Presence of { *George Jones* / *Eliza Coleman* }

No. 65.

James Powell of *this* Parish *Bachelor* and *Mary Williams* of *this* Parish *Spinster* were married in this *Church* by *Banns* ~~with Consent of~~ this *thirteenth* Day of *May* in the Year One thousand eight hundred and *thirty four* By me *Thomas William Webb, Curate*

This Marriage was solemnized between us { *James Powell* X his mark / *Mary Williams* X her mark }

In the Presence of { *Joseph Elliott* / *Thomas Yeomans* }

No. 66.

A typical example of a post-1754 (Hardwick's) marriage register from St Weonard's, Herefordshire, 1834; the original is at the Herefordshire Record Office.

(4) **Other county marriage and burial indexes** are being compiled by local family history societies and individuals. Several counties are completely covered. Although not normally accessible for personal searches, these indexes may usually be searched for quite small fees. They are listed with the fees involved in *Marriage and Census Indexes for Family Historians*, J. Gibson & E. Hampson (Federation of Family History Societies, 8th edn. 2000). Some can be accessed online through a pay-per-view online service at www.familyhistoryonline.net, published by the Federation of Family History Societies.

It cannot be too strongly stressed that in each and every case where entries are found in indexes of this kind they should be checked and the full details obtained from the original registers. The main indexes are not complete and no conclusion should be drawn solely from the evidence that they contain. The original registers of the places from which your ancestors came should always be searched over wide periods and the burial registers should never be neglected. Each ancestor's death or burial should always be sought out and recorded before you proceed to search back for details of the earlier generation. The age at death may indicate an approximate date of birth. If the death of a widow cannot be found, remember that she may have remarried and changed her name.

It is unfortunate that the register entries themselves are frequently very un-informative but they must still be looked at. A baptism will normally give the forenames of both parents (but not the maiden name of the mother). A marriage before 1837 will usually only show the names of the parties involved and not their ages or the names of their parents (though the names of the two witnesses recorded after 1754 may be useful). A burial before 1813 will only show the age of the deceased if one is comparatively lucky. Occupations rarely appear.

Useful summary lists of England and Welsh parishes, showing the whereabouts of their parish registers, the availability of copies and the extent to which they are covered by the above indexes, are published in *The Phillimore Atlas and Index of Parish Registers*, C.R. Humphery-Smith (Phillimore, 3rd edn. 2002).

Scottish parish registers

Most Scottish parish registers before 1855 are at New Register House, Princes Street, Edinburgh EH1 3YT. Few begin before 1750 but all the baptisms and marriages (but not the burials) prior to 1855 have been indexed by the Genealogical Society of Utah. The indexes to these 'Old Parochial Registers' (OPRs) are arranged by county and are available on microfiche at various libraries and Family History Centres. There is a set at the Society of Genealogists. Indexes to the OPR baptisms and proclamations/ marriages can be viewed online at www.scotlandspeople.gov.uk.

Welsh parish registers

The above comments about English registers generally apply, but for the whereabouts of Welsh parish registers see *Parish Registers of Wales*, C.J. Williams & J. Watts-Williams (Society of Genealogists, National Index of Parish Registers, Vol. 13, 1986).

Irish parish registers

Many Irish registers have not survived. In the rural areas those which have survived date only from the early nineteenth century. In the Republic of Ireland the Church of Ireland (i.e. Anglican church) registers before 1870 are public records. Most are still held by the local clergy, but some have been deposited in the National Archives of Ireland and others are at the Representative Church Body Library, Braemor Park, Churchtown, Dublin 14. (Tel: 00 353 1 492 3979; www.ireland.anglican.org/library). Catholic parish registers are normally still held by the parish priest, but there are microfilms of most prior to 1880 in the National Archives, Bishop Street, Dublin 8. (Tel: 00 353 1 407 2300; www.nationalarchives.ie). Records from parishes in Northern Ireland, which are not retained in parish custody, are deposited in the Public Record Office of Northern Ireland, 66 Balmoral Avenue, Belfast BT9 6NY (Tel: 028 902 5905; www.proni.gov.uk). See *Guide to Irish Parish Registers*, B. Mitchell (Baltimore, 1988) or *Irish Records: Sources for Family and Local History*, J. Ryan (Flyleaf Press, Dublin, 3rd edn. 2003). Many Irish registers have been indexed by government supported local Heritage Centres. Contact details are given by the *Irish Times* (see http://scripts.ireland.com/ancestor/browse/addresses).

Nonconformist registers

If the family did not attend the Church of England, its baptisms may be found in the registers of a nonconformist chapel. Few families remained staunchly Anglican and if expected events cannot be found in the Church of England registers, then nonconformity should always be considered. Microfilms of most surviving nonconformist registers in England and Wales before 1837 are at the Family Records Centre (see 'Civil registration' above), but others remain in the various chapels or are deposited with the denominational headquarters or at the appropriate county record office.

The baptisms in the registers at the Family Records Centre have been indexed into the International Genealogical Index (IGI). Three important groups of nonconformist registers deposited at the National Archives, however, are not yet included in that Index. They are (1) the births and marriages of Quakers 1650s–1837, (2) the births and baptisms of Baptists, Congregationalists and Presbyterians registered at Dr. William's Registry 1743–1837, and (3) the births and baptisms of Wesleyans registered at the Wesleyan Metropolitan Registry 1818–1841. Items (2) and (3) have been indexed onto the *British Isles Vital Records Index* CDs published as supplements to the IGI on CD-ROM.

Few nonconformist marriages, other than of Quakers and Jews, took place in England and Wales before 1837, and the marriages of Baptists, Catholics, Congregationalists, Methodists and English Presbyterians between 1754 and 1837 are normally found in Church of England registers. Catholics may, however, also have gone through private ceremonies that may have been recorded separately by the priests involved. Some Catholic registers before 1837 are at the Family Records Centre (and are included in the IGI) but others remain in the churches or have been deposited in local record offices. See *Catholic Missions and Registers 1700–1880*, M.J.

Gandy (1993, 6 parts), which gives details of all known registers in England, Wales, Scotland, the Channel Islands and the Isle of Man.

Research back to 1837 should basically be carried out through the normal records of civil registration and the census returns. Once you have arrived at that date there are several volumes in the *My Ancestors…* series published by the Society of Genealogists which will be helpful: *My Ancestors were Baptists*, G.R. Breed (4th edn. 2002); *My Ancestors were Congregationalists*, D.J.H. Clifford (2nd edn. 1997); *My Ancestors were Jewish*, A. Joseph (3rd edn. 2002); *My Ancestors were Methodists*, W. Leary (2nd edn. 1999); *My Ancestors were English Presbyterians/Unitarians*, A. Ruston (2001); *My Ancestors were Quakers*, E.H. Milligan & M.J. Thomas (2nd edn, 1999) and *My ancestors were Inghamites*, P.J. Oates (2003).

The surviving nonconformist registers of Wales are listed in *Nonconformist Registers of Wales*, D. Ifans (National Library of Wales and Welsh County Archivists Group, 1994).

Society of Genealogists

At this stage of your research it will be worth your while to visit the Society of Genealogists at 14 Charterhouse Buildings, Goswell Road, London EC1M 7BA (Tel. 020 7251 8799; open Tuesday, Wednesday, Friday, Saturday 10.00–6.00, Thursday 10.00–8.00; www.sog.org.uk).

You need not be a member of the Society, as the Library is open to searchers at a minimum charge (currently) of £3.50 for one hour, £9.20 for four hours or £14.50 for the day. No appointment is necessary. If you wish to stay all day there is a common room with a drinks machine for those bringing sandwiches.

If you join, you also benefit from the quarterly *Genealogists' Magazine*, discounts on the Society's publications, on lectures and seminars and on the courses for beginners. Members can access various Society collections and indexes remotely via www.englishorigins.com free of charge four times a year. Members in the British Isles may also borrow printed books, microfilms and microfiche, with certain exceptions. The membership fee is currently £40 a year and there is in addition an entrance fee of £10 payable on first joining.

An outline guide to the contents and use of the Library is available on the website www.sog.org.uk, which also gives guidance on finding the Society along with information leaflets and other news of the Society. Free tours of the Library are held every other Saturday and these can be booked in the Library by calling 020 7702 5485 or emailing library@sog.org.uk. The Library, which was started in 1911 and has over 100,000 volumes as well as much manuscript, electronic and microform material, is arranged on three floors with each floor having a general theme:

Sources for places in the United Kingdom:

(a) **Middle Library or British Isles Collection:** here on the first floor the shelves are arranged in alphabetical order of the old English counties from Bedfordshire to Yorkshire, followed by Scotland, Wales, the Isle of Man and the Channel Islands. The books in each section are divided into eight groups:

(1) General works about the area and its records, such as bibliographies, histories, maps, newspapers, place names, record office guides, heralds' visitations and Wills. For some areas there are large manuscript collections and indexes compiled by previous genealogists. These include Snell's Berkshire Collection, Rogers' Cornish Pedigrees and Boyd's Citizens of London. The Macleod Collection for Scotland is on the basement archive area of the Lower Library. The Welply Collection of Irish Will abstracts can be found in the Upper Library.

(2) Local histories and other topographical material, parish histories and church guides.

(3) Parish registers. The Society has the largest collection of copies of parish registers in the country (about 10,000) including an almost complete series of all that have ever been printed and hundreds in typescript and manuscript. The parishes and dates covered (the earliest being 1538 and the latest generally 1837 although some may continue into the last century) are listed in the various *County Guides* published by the Society or can be found on the website www.sog.org.uk. The collection and the published catalogue include more than 600 nonconformist registers. There is full coverage for Scotland before 1855 and much Isle of Man and Guernsey material.

(4) Monumental inscriptions. The inscriptions on the tombstones in a large number of churchyards have been copied. Many are listed in the various *County Sources Guides* published by the Society. Tombstone inscriptions (though not always accurate, particularly where ages are concerned) are one of the most obvious sources of genealogical information. Many local family history societies have made great efforts to record all the inscriptions in their areas and county record offices may have copies of others that no longer survive made by antiquaries in the past.

(5) Censuses. The Society holds many copies of the Census Returns 1841–91, especially for the 1851 and 1891 censuses, and there is complete coverage for 1881. Some counties are covered in other years. There is a large collection of indexes to the names in them. There is a published catalogue, *Census Copies and Indexes in the Library of the Society of Genealogists* (3rd edn., 1995). Internet access is available to use the 1881, 1891 and 1901 indexes published online.

(6) Directories and poll books. Poll books show the names of those who voted in parliamentary elections between 1694 and 1832. Trade directories for many provincial towns have been published regularly from the 1770s and may contain alphabetical, classified and street lists. Similar national and county directories exist from the 1780s and grow in detail from the 1840s. There is a published catalogue, *Directories and Poll Books in the Library of the Society of Genealogists* (6th edn. 1995).

(7) Periodicals. These are the publications of the local record and archaeological societies and of all the local family history societies in the British Isles.

There is a published catalogue of the whole of the Scottish (1996) and Irish (2000) collections, and specific county guides listing registers, monumental inscriptions and marriage licences for all English Counties and all of Wales.

Sources for what research has been done before, what people did and foreign research:

(b) **Upper Library:** in this room on the second floor the main collections are:

   (1) Family Histories. An extensive collection of bound printed, typescript and manuscript family histories and one-name studies.

   (2) Schools and Universities. Registers of public and other schools and of the ancient British universities and colleges. There is a published catalogue, *School, University and College Registers and Histories in the Library of the Society of Genealogists* (1996).

   (3) Apprentices of Great Britain 1710–1774. The record of the collection of tax on apprenticeship indentures. In two alphabetical series 1710–1762 and 1762–1774, with indexes of the masters.

   (4) Professions. The series includes good runs of Army and Navy Lists and of the Medical Register with material on other professions arranged in alphabetical order. The maritime material here and else wherein the Library is listed in *Maritime Sources in the Library of the Society of Genealogists* (1997).

   (5) Boyd's Marriage Index (see 'Parish registers' above).

   (6) Heraldry, Royalty, Peerage, Biography. There are extensive runs of Burke's Peerage and Burke's Landed Gentry, Debrett's Peerage, Walford's County Families and older peerages.

   (7) Religions. Includes a run of Crockford's Clerical Directory, material on the various nonconformist denominations, the publications of the Catholic Record Society, the Huguenot Society, the Jewish Historical Society and other related works.

   (8) Wills. Many indexes of Wills are located in the Middle Library, but those which cover more than one county are here. The Society has indexes for nearly all the ancient probate courts in England and Wales from the sixteenth century or earlier to 1858, many on microfilm. They are described in *Will Indexes and Other Probate Material in the Library of the Society of Genealogists* (1996).

   (9) Marriage Licences. Many indexes of marriage licences are located in the Middle Library, but those which cover more than one county are here. See *Marriage Licences: Abstracts and Indexes in the Library of the Society of Genealogists* (4th edn. 1991).

   (10) Genealogical Periodicals and Public Records.

   (11) Overseas. Collections of material on British people living abroad, in the Commonwealth and in America, are maintained. They include many indexes of passenger lists of people going to America before 1900.

Periodicals are received from numerous genealogical societies worldwide. Material on the British in India is listed in *Sources for Anglo-Indian Genealogy in the Library of the Society of Genealogists* (1990).

Sources for beginners and unique collections:

(c) **Lower Library:** in the room on the lower ground floor there is a microfilm collection of over 11,500 reels and much microfiche material, the computer suite items where one can use the Internet, CD-ROMs and other electronic media. The main items being as follows:

(1) General Register Office, indexes of births, marriages and deaths in England and Wales 1837–1926, on microfiche.

(2) Indexes of births, marriages and deaths in Scotland, 1855–1920, on microfilm, and complete indexes of baptisms and marriages contained in the Old Parochial Registers before 1855 on microfiche.

(3) The FamilySearch database can be found on CD-ROM on the computers (also networked onto other floors) and there is Internet access to www.familysearch.org which includes the International Genealogical Index, Ancestral File and other databases. The 1992 edition on microfiche remains in a microfiche cabinet for those who do not wish to use computers.

(4) Principal Probate Registry, microfilm indexes of Wills and administrations for England and Wales 1858–1930. Microfilm copies of abstracts of Wills collected by the Bank of England 1717–1945 and a few miscellaneous copies of some Wills proved in the Prerogative Court of Canterbury. Microfilm copies of the indexes to Wills recorded in the Estate Duty Office Registers.

(5) *The Times*, indexes of births, marriages and deaths reported in *The Times* 1785–1933 (with the announcements themselves to 1920) on microfilm. There are yearly manuscript indexes to the deaths 1894–1931 and a copy of *Palmers Index to the Times 1790–1905 on CD-ROM* is networked on the computers.

(6) Bernau Index. An index on microfilm of Chancery and other Court proceedings containing about four and a half million references prior to 1800. See *How to Use the Bernau Index* (Society of Genealogists, 2000).

(7) Indexes on CD-ROM and microfiche of births, marriages and deaths in Australia to 1902 (later for some states) and in New Zealand 1848–1920.

(8) Document Collection. The large collection contains miscellaneous manuscripts research notes (pedigrees, Will abstracts, notes and letters) donated by members and others, and is arranged by surname and place name. Material received since February 1992 is on microfiche in alphabetical order by surname.

(9) Special Collections. These are generally manuscript notes on families that have not been split up by surname as the collections deal with families connected by specific subjects, such as Huguenots or Jewish

families, or by what they did, such as civil servants or teachers. Some of the collections have been microfilmed to conserve them. Included amongst the special collections are thousands of manuscript roll pedigrees or family trees. Most are indexed by name in the card index to the Special Collections.

(10) A microfilm copy has been made of the miscellaneous slip index, known as the Great Card Index, with about three million references, mainly relating to London and the South East of England prior to 1800 but containing a wide variety of other material.

(11) Computer suite. All items requiring use of a computer such as CD-ROMs and Internet access are available in the lower library. Free access is given to some pay per view or subscription sites such as www.englishorigins.com or www.ancestry.co.uk.

The Society actively organises and encourages the transcription of parish registers and monumental inscriptions and seeks to provide a clearing house for information on the whereabouts of copies of both.

The Society's own publications can be found in the publication sales area on the ground floor. This is open Tuesday, Wednesday, Friday and Saturday 10.00–6.00 and Thursday 10.00–8.00. The Society is generally closed in the first full week of February. For up-to-date lists of Society publications, bookshop stock, or microfiche and maps for sale, send a stamped addressed envelope or two International Reply Coupons. Alternatively, you may visit the website www.sog.org.uk.

County record offices and libraries

When you have exhausted the records of civil registration and census returns and have begun to look at the parish registers of the area from which your family came from, you will need to consult the other sources available in the county record office.

Each county has at least one county record office supported by the local authority. It may have a close connection with a local studies library. Like county libraries the record offices are often open without charge, though fees are charged in the offices at Exeter, Gloucester and Lincoln. When visiting a library or record office for the first time always contact it in advance to make sure that they have the records you require, to check the opening hours and, when necessary, to book a seat or a microfilm or microfiche reader. Evidence of identity and address or a reader's ticket may be required. Most county record offices will have a website containing all the above information. Use the Historical Manuscript Commission's Archon Directory which includes links to all record offices at www.hmc.gov.uk/archon. If a guide to the office's contents has been published, this will make a good starting point so that when you go you have a clear idea of what searches you intend to carry out. If you have several alternative research strategies, you will not then be disappointed to have gone a long way only to find that you do not have sufficient things to occupy your time. When visiting or writing to a record office please bear in mind the points made in 'Some words of advice' below.

The main records used by genealogists in county record offices are:

(1) Census returns (see 'Census returns 1841–1901' above). The copies found locally are listed in *Census Returns 1841–1891 on Microfilm*, J. Gibson (Federation of Family History Societies, 6th edn. 2002). Most will have also purchased copies of the 1901 census for there area and many provide Internet access to the National Archives online index.

(2) Parish registers (see 'Parish registers'). The county record office will always have the latest details of the whereabouts of any register in the county. Copies are now normally provided on microfilm or microfiche and in a few counties they are available through the local county library system. Also at the record office will be the annual copies of the parish registers called 'bishops' transcripts' and the local licences issued for marriages, both of which may provide variant or additional material.

(3) Other parish records, varying in quantity but perhaps including the accounts of churchwardens and of the overseers of the poor and papers about the legal place of 'settlement' of poor people. There may also be workhouse records and, after 1834, records of the Poor Law Unions.

(4) Wills proved in the local church courts before 1858. See *Probate Jurisdictions: Where to Look for Wills*, J. Gibson & E. Churchill (Federation of Family History Societies, 5th edn. 2002). Do not forget to consult the indexes to the Wills proved in the Prerogative Court of Canterbury as well (see 'The National Archives' above).

(5) The records of the administration of the county will include Land Tax records showing owners and occupiers, at least from 1780. The quarter session records will include the various activities of the Justices of the Peace in administering the poor laws, licences, local crime, etc. See *Quarter Session Records for Family Historians*, J. Gibson (Federation of Family History Societies, 4th edn. 1995) and *Land and Window Tax Assessments*, J. Gibson, M. Medlycott & D. Mills (Federation of Family History Societies, 2nd edn, 1998).

(6) Record offices and some larger libraries may have files of electoral registers, perhaps going back to 1832, arranged by street and not by name.

(7) Directories. Trade directories were published in many towns from the 1770s onwards and for country areas from the 1820s. They may help to locate a family in the Census Returns.

(8) Newspapers. Sets of local newspapers may be found in county record offices or libraries. Only a few are indexed by name. If they cannot be seen locally, there will be copies at the British Library Newspaper Library, Colindale Avenue, London NW9 5HE (Tel. 020 7412 7353). See *Local Newspapers 1750–1920: A Select Location List*, J. Gibson, B. Langston & B.W. Smith (Federation of Family History Societies, 2nd edn.2002). Large reference libraries may have *The Times* on microfilm, together with its printed indexes. These indexes do not include the reported births, marriages and deaths, and for indexes to them see 'Society of Genealogists' above.

(9) Maps. Many local libraries and record offices have early editions of Ordnance Survey maps or will know where copies of the six-inch-to-the-mile maps may be seen. Record offices may have other manuscript maps including 'enclosure awards' showing fields and commons in the eighteenth and nineteenth centuries and tithe maps (between 1836 and 1860), that predated Ordnance Survey maps, both providing the names of owners and occupiers of land.

(10) Schools. The existence of a local school can be ascertained from the brief descriptions of villages found in trade directories and if its registers survive, they will be at the school or at the county record office. Universal elementary education did not start until 1870 and even after that date it seems that more log books of incidental events survive than registers of pupils.

(11) Apprentices. The drawing up of apprenticeship indentures (i.e. contracts) involved trouble and expense and most working children were trained without such formality. To make matters worse indentures were private documents and most have not survived. Those indentures which were taxed are recorded in a series of ledgers at the National Archives, Kew, 1710–1804, but they do not show parentage after about 1750. There are indexes 1710–1774 at the Society of Genealogists. At county record offices you may find some record of poor apprentices paid for by their parishes between 1601 and 1834 or by some local charity and in borough record offices there may be a record of apprentices in a company or guild or in the borough itself.

(12) Records of local land or estate owners and of local businesses.

Addresses and opening hours of county record libraries are given in the official *Record Repositories in Great Britain* (Historical Manuscripts Commisson, 11th edn. 1999). Many of the indexes of names to be found in county record offices are listed in *Specialist Indexes for Family Historians*, J. Gibson & E Hampson (Federation of Family History Societies, 2nd edn. 2000).

This Manual has only mentioned a few of the printed books which are of assistance to family historians and which are to be found in public libraries. An excellent survey of the wide variety available is *Genealogy for Librarians*, R. Harvey (Library Association Publishing, London, 2nd edn. 1992) or *Using Libraries: Workshops for Family Historians*, S. Raymond (Federation of Family History Societies, 2001).

Little of this material is available for home reading and so a certain amount of travelling will be inevitable, though photocopies can sometimes be provided. There is no right to have photocopies and if this is likely to damage the book or manuscript or, indeed, to infringe copyright, then the custodian has a responsibility to see that no photocopying is carried out.

Local family history societies

In addition to the Society of Genealogists there are many local family history societies. Membership of the one in your area and of those where your family came from may be helpful. They have regular meetings and talks, undertake valuable transcription and indexing work and produce quarterly journals and other publications. If you join one of these societies, details of the families in which you are interested may usually be published in its journal without charge.

Many local societies have compiled indexes of marriages in their areas, of monumental inscriptions, census returns and other records. The societies will usually undertake postal searches in these indexes in return for small fees. These indexes and the fees charged are listed in *Marriage and Census Indexes for Family Historians*, J. Gibson & E. Hampson (Federation of Family History Societies, 8th edn. 2000).

Some local societies have extensive publishing programmes of basic indexes and other material for their areas. Those works available are listed in two publications of the Federation of Family History Societies' *Current Publications by Member Societies* (10th edn. 1999) and *Current Publications by Member Societies on Microfiche* (5th edn. 2002 published on CD-ROM). Many local societies sell their publications through Family History Books (Incorporating GenFair) – the online bookshop of the Federation of Family History Societies – FFHS Publications Ltd., Units 15–16, Chesham Industrial Centre, Oram Street, Bury BL9 6EN (Tel. 0161 797 3843; www.ffhs.co.uk).

Although you may not have ancestors in the area where you now live, there are several advantages in joining the local society. You will be able to see the exchange journals received from many other local societies, not only in the British Isles but from overseas as well. There will also be a basic reference library and a bookstall as well as periodic lectures about sources in general.

As mentioned above (see 'Is somebody else working on this family?') full details of most societies worldwide, including subscription rates, will be found in the annually published *Genealogical Research Directory*.

The majority of the local family history societies in England and Wales and many overseas belong to the Federation of Family History Societies (FFHS). An up-to-date list of addresses of these societies may be obtained from its Administrator, PO Box 2425, Coventry CV5 6YX or by emailing admin@ffhs.org.uk; it is published twice-yearly in its journal *Family History News & Digest*. The Federation's website (www.ffhs.org.uk) includes a list of all member societies with contact postal addresses, email addresses and website addresses with links. The Federation itself has no library and does not undertake research. However, it maintains an online pay-per-view database of many of the indexes and finding aids (notably marriage, census and burial indexes) compiled by constituent members. The site containing nearly 18 million records can be found on www.familyhistoryonline.net. Details of local societies in Scotland may be obtained from the website of the Scottish Association of Family History Societies (SAFHS) at www.safhs.org.uk.

The National Archives

The National Archives (TNA) bring together the former Public Record Office (PRO) and the Historical Manuscript Commission (HMC). TNA houses the records of central government and the law courts from Domesday Book in 1086 to the present century. Staff do not undertake genealogical research. The National Archives website gives excellent information about the archives including information leaflets, catalogues and some online documents on www.nationalarchives.gov.uk.

The search rooms are located at the National Archives, Ruskin Avenue, Kew, Richmond, Surrey TW9 4DU (Tel. 020 8876 3444). They are open to the public from 9.00–5.00 on Monday, Wednesday and Friday; 10.00–7.00 on Tuesday; 9.00–7.00 on Thursday and 9.30–5.00 on Saturday, except for public holidays and during the annual stock-taking week generally at the end of November or the beginning of December.

A reader's ticket must be obtained in order to see original records and is issued on production of some means of identification, such as a banker's card, or for foreign nationals, a passport or some other form of national identification document.

Many documents that refer to individuals are closed for 100 years in order to safeguard personal confidentiality and no public record is normally made available until 30 years after the date of its final creation.

A group of records heavily used by genealogists has been made available in central London on the first floor of the Family Records Centre (see 'Civil registration' and 'Census returns 1841–1901' above). These consist only of microform copies of the census returns 1841–1901, the Wills and administrations before 1858 from the Prerogative Court of Canterbury, the Estate Duty Office death duty registers 1796–1858 and the non-parochial registers 1567–1858. No reader's ticket is needed for the consultation of this material.

The main records used by genealogists at Kew are probably those of personnel in the services and professions. For further details see the guides mentioned below which should be consulted prior to any visit. They include:

(a) Army: see *Army Records for Family Historians*, S. Fowler and W. Spencer (National Archives, 1998); and *Army Service Records of the First World War*, W. Spencer (National Archives, 3rd edn. 2001).

(b) Navy: see *Using Navy Records (Public Record Office Pocket Guide)*, B. Pappalardo (National Archives, 2001) and *Tracing Your Navy Ancestors*, B. Pappalardo (National Archives, 2002).

(c) Merchant seamen: see *My Ancestor was a Merchant Seaman*, C.T. & M.J. Watts (Society of Genealogists, 2002).

(d) Marines from 1793: see *Records of the Royal Marines*, G. Thomas (National Archives, 1994).

(e) Royal Air Force: see *The Records of the Royal Air Force; How to Find the Few*, E. Wilson (Federation of Family History Societies, 1991) and *Air Force Records for Family Historians*, W. Spencer (National Archives, 2000).

(f) Coastguards from 1816 to 1923.

(g) Customs officers from 1683 and excisemen from 1696.

(h) Metropolitan Police from 1829 (except 1857–1869): see *My Ancestor was a Policeman*, A. Sherman (Society of Genealogists, 2000).

(i) Railway staff registers from 1835: see *Was Your Grandfather a Railwayman?*, T. Richards (Federation of Family History Societies, 3rd edn. 1995); *Railway Ancestors: A Guide to the Staff Records of the Railway Companies of England and Wales 1822–1947*, D.T. Hawkings (Public Record Office & Sutton Publishing, 1995) and *Railway Records*, C. Edwards (National Archives, 2001).

(j) Solicitors' articles of clerkship 1730–1875.

(k) Clergy institutions to benefices 1556–1838.

Records of postmen 1737–1940 are not at the National Archives but at Postal Heritage Trust, Freeling House, Phoenix Place, London WC1X 0DL (Tel. 020 7239 2570).

Records of civil and criminal litigation are also held at Kew. For these, the general guide mentioned below should be consulted but for criminals see also *Criminal Ancestors; A Guide to Historical Criminal Records in England and Wales*, D.T. Hawkings (Sutton Publishing, 1996).

First-time visitors to the National Archives are strongly advised to read *New to Kew?*, J. Cox (National Archives, 1997) but for fuller details see *Tracing your Ancestors in the Public Record Office*, A. Bevan (National Archives, 6th edn. 2002) and S. Colwell, *Dictionary of Genealogical Sources in the Public Record Office* (1992).

There are hundreds of free information leaflets on sources at the National Archives available through the website www.nationalarchives.gov.uk.

Family History Centres

Family History Centres are branches of the Family History Library in Salt Lake City, Utah. They are usually located in the meeting houses of the Church of Jesus Christ of Latter-Day Saints (LDS) but they are open without charge or formality to any member of the public.

Each centre has copies of the International Genealogical Index (see 'Parish registers' above) and the Family History Library Catalogue, i.e. the catalogue of the library in Salt Lake City. If the centre has the International Genealogical Index on CD-ROM as part of the group of programs called 'FamilySearch' it will normally also have the program called 'Ancestral File' which contains details of a further 29 million people linked in 11 million families. Supplements to the CDs have been published as the *British Isles Vital Records Index* and *Pedigree Resource Files*, adding millions more entries to the databases. Many of the latter will contain unedited notes and sources related to lineage-linked pedigrees that have been submitted to the LDS mainly by Americans. The CDs may be purchased from the Garretts Green Distribution Centre or from the website below. Another section of FamilySearch which is of great value in tracing families in America is the Social Security Death Index which provides details of over 50 million people who have died in America since 1937. The centres may also have reference sources and copies of some records.

At these centres it is possible to carry out a remarkable range of research by borrowing microfilm or microfiche copies of records from Salt Lake City, chosen from the Family History Library Catalogue. A small fee is charged. Thus, if you have ancestors or family, for instance, in Germany or America you may be able to see the records involved without the necessity of going to those countries.

The centres are staffed by volunteers and they vary in their opening hours. Details of all the Family History Centres are listed on www.familysearch.org. A list of those in the British Isles may be obtained from the Family History Support Office, 185 Penns Lane, Sutton Coldfield, Birmingham B76 1JU (Tel. 0121 784 1460). The address of your nearest centre will be found in the phone book under 'Church of Jesus Christ of Latter-Day Saints'. Always telephone in advance to check opening hours; the Centres will not normally answer inquiries by post.

Some words of advice

Always remember that the documents used by family historians were not created for that purpose. The previous sections have outlined the common sources that can help in starting family history research. However far back you research, it is important to remember the reason why a document was created. Who wrote it and who is it about? Would the person concerned have given the information himself or herself? Would he or she have been able to read it? Levels of literacy were quite low. Not everyone would have attended school until quite late into the nineteenth century and a significant number of people may not have been able to read, or write their own name.

The spelling of a name often depended on how the writer heard it. Hence spellings of names can cause problems, especially when relying on name indexes rather than the document itself. It can be dangerous to disregard other spelling variants of a name or to insist that one's family only ever used a particular spelling. The surname FUELL can be spelt FEWELL, KNOTT can be spelt NOTT and in either case the double letter at the end may not always appear. The name CLOUGH sounds like CLUFF and PHALING sounds like FALING. An antiquated form of the name ARMSTRONG can be STRONGITHARM. Pet names or shortened versions of forenames might mislead. Lou might mean Louise or Lucy. Bert might be short for Albert, Bertram or Herbert. Aliases or name changes may confuse. Not all changes of name are recorded, as the common law entitles a person to call himself what he wishes. Place names might be mistaken especially when found in a census. Leeds might well mean Leeds in Yorkshire but there is also a Leeds in Kent. Dialect can influence how a place name might be heard. A census enumerator in Wales clearly wrote down what he heard when the head of the household gave his birth place as ATNUTSFORD rather than NUTSFORD in Cheshire. If there is any ambiguity then check an atlas or contemporary gazetteer.

Handwriting styles can be difficult to get used to. Only practice will get one used to the unusual letter forms in which the letters 'ss' might be written as 'f', or 'th' written as 'y'. Often words might be written as a 'contraction' or shortened form in documents. Learn to recognise common words and phrases that are bound to appear in a specific document, so that you can readily recognise specific letters as they appear elsewhere. Learn to read roman numerals and remember the old terms used for money – it is surprising how easy it has been to forget pounds, shillings and pence.

Vocabulary can be very different from today. Definitions can be found in the dictionary of archaic words but these may vary according to time and local custom. The following terms appear quite often in parish registers and Wills:

- Yeoman (a freeholder who worked his own land)
- Husbandman (a tenant who worked on rented land)
- Journeyman (day labourer)
- Sojourner (a temporary resident)
- Relict (widow)

Family terms may not always be used as they are today. Father might mean father-in-law or step-father just as cousin might mean any relative, even one by marriage.

Many records and some legal documents before 1733 might be in Latin or a mixture of English and Latin. Often the Latin form of a Christian name is recorded in registers for example 'Jacobus' for James or 'Guliemus' for William. Common terms found in registers also include:

- bastard   *illigitimus*
- born   *natus*
- buried   *sepultar*
- daughter   *filia*
- father   *pater*
- mother   *mater*
- son   *filius*
- widow   *vidua*
- wife   *uxor*

Dates in early documents can be confusing. Before 1752, the New Year in England followed the Julian calendar and the year started on 25 March. When the Gregorian calendar was introduced in 1752 the year was established as starting on 1 January and the terms 'Old Style' and 'New Style' came into use when quoting dates. Thus the date 15 February 1715 (Old Style) would be quoted as '15 February 1716 (New Style)'. If the day fell after 24 March, the year, of course, was the same. Documents often give both the Old Style and the New Style year, e.g. '23 January 1741/2' (1741 Old Style, 1742 New Style). However, after 1752 only one calendar was in use in the UK and the necessity of specifying dates as 'Old' or 'New' style disappeared.

The change of the year-end in 1752 required the 'one off' removal of eleven days from the year, between 2 and 14 September 1752. Thus 1752 was eleven days shorter than any other year (so you should not – in theory – find any English documents dated 3 to 13 September 1752). The following table might help:

Julian/Gregorian Calendar
Old style/New style

NOV	1750	
DEC	1750	
JAN	1750/51	OS/NS

FEB	1750/51	OS/NS
MAR 24	1750/51	OS/NS
MAR 25	1751	
APR	1751	
MAY	1751	
JUN	1751	
JUL	1751	
AUG	1751	
SEP	1751	
OCT	1751	
NOV	1751	
DEC	1751	
JAN	1751/52	OS/NS
FEB	1751/52	OS/NS
MAR 24	1751/52	OS/NS
MAR 25	1752	
MAY	1752	
JUN	1752	
JUL	1752	
AUG	1752	
SEP 2/14	1752	
OCT	1752	
NOV	1752	
DEC	1752	
JAN	1753	
FEB	1753	
MAR	1753	
APR	1753	

It has been truly said that genealogy is basically a do-it-yourself pastime. You may be lucky and discover relatives who are tracing the same lines and who are willing to share their information, but the greatest satisfaction comes from the slow assemblage of facts over a period of time and from personal research.

A family history is not something which can be put together in a few months, let alone a few weeks or hours. It may take a good deal of time. Success will depend to a large extent on the social status of the family you are tracing, on the frequency of its surname, on the way in which it moves about and changes its occupation and, inevitably, on the extent to which the appropriate records have survived. Many genealogists, it has to be said, encounter problems in the nineteenth century and are immediately discouraged.

However, although your family may be uniquely interesting the problems you have in tracing it will be the same as those of any other genealogist. That is why reading about the subject in different textbooks and meeting other genealogists through your local family history society can be very worthwhile. Many societies (including the Society of Genealogists) run lectures, workshops and courses on specific records or research techniques that will be beneficial.

It is not fair, however, to expect librarians and record office staff to take a personal interest in your searches, however intensely interesting and exciting they may be.

There are many thousands of genealogists and they have put a great strain on the services and goodwill of archivists and librarians, not only in the British Isles, but worldwide. Lengthy letters, emails, telephone calls and conversation may be met with polite interest, but please remember that they detract from the main work of any office.

Always, therefore, keep any enquiry as short as possible and make sure, before you send it, that the answer is not easily available by personal visit to your local public library. This is where access to the website, library and bookstall of your local family history society can be so useful.

It is also well to remember, when asking for information from anyone, private or official, that there may be no reply unless you provide an addressed envelope with appropriate stamps (or, for correspondents abroad, International Reply Coupons obtainable from Post Offices).

The Society of Genealogists receives many thousands of enquiries every year. When answering questions the staff and volunteers often find themselves asking key questions to draw out the information they need to help answer the problem. Think about those key questions below when trying to solve your research problems:

WHOM are you looking for?
- is the name correct?
- note spelling variations
- could this be a nickname or alias?
- could there be a change of name?
- type of person – will affect the search –
    - agricultural labourer
    - middle class professional
    - land owner or pauper?

WHAT are you looking for?
- birth/baptism, marriage, death/burial
- supplementary evidence (e.g. marriage licences, banns)
- what did they do?
    - practice a particular profession, trade?
    - migrate?

WHERE are you looking?
- look at a map, develop a sense of place
- where would you expect the event to have taken place?
- is it a parish – small rural parish or urban town with many churches?
- is a county-/country- wide search practical
- International Genealogical Index (IGI) covers many parishes
- see www.familysearch.org
- localise the name using county-wide indexes
    - e.g. marriage, burial or census indexes

London attracts lots of people –
>   Pallot's Marriage Index 1780–1837
>   Boyd's Inhabitants of London 16th–18th centuries

consider transport links

where is the nearest large market town?

remember our ancestors were not restricted by county boundaries

records could be in another record office

WHEN are you looking?

before or after 1837 will usually mean searching in civil records or parish registers

alive after 1851 means the age and place of birth might be found in a census

when was the first known child born?

marriages often take place shortly afterwards or sometimes much earlier

get different evidences of age – this can vary from source to source

think of the types of records relevant to the time period –
>   e.g. apprenticeships more likely to be found in the 1700s when they were taxed, than the 1900s when they were less regulated hence unrecorded

WHY are you looking?

think laterally but stay focussed

remember why you started this search

will another source give similar information?
>   e.g. marriage certificates give age so do you need the birth certificate?

will a sibling's birth certificate give the same information?

death certificates give evidence of age but the informant may not be reliable

Professional assistance

If you yourself are not in a position to trace your family, or if you need help in distant parts of the United Kingdom or with documents in Latin or in difficult handwriting, there are professional searchers who undertake such work.

The Association of Genealogists and Researchers in Archives (AGRA) was founded in 1968 to promote high standards among professional genealogists. The Association maintains 'A List of Members' showing the geographical and subject areas of their expertise that can be found on its website www.agra.org.uk. The Society of Genealogists also publishes a leaflet, *Employing a Professional Researcher: A Practical Guide* freely available from its website.

A list of professionals in Scotland may be obtained from the Association of Scottish Genealogists and Record Agents (ASGRA), 51/3 Mortonhall Road, Edinburgh EH9 2HN or from its website www.asgra.co.uk, and in Ireland from the Association of Professional Genealogists in Ireland (APGI), c/o the Honorary Secretary, 30 Harlech Crescent, Clonskeagh, Dublin 14, Eire (http://indigo.ie/~apgi).

Bibliography

Air Force Records for Family Historians, W. Spencer (National Archives, 2000)

Ancestors, The National Archives, PO Box 38, Richmond, Surrey TW9 4AJ

Ancestral Trails: The Complete Guide to British Genealogy and Family History, M.D. Herber (Sutton Publishing, Stroud, 2nd edn. 2004)

Army Records for Family Historians, S. Fowler & W. Spencer (National Archives, 1998)

Army Service Records of the First World War, W. Spencer (National Archives, 3rd edn. 2001)

Bibliography of Irish Family History, E. MacLysaght (Dublin, 1982)

Bibliography of Irish Family History and Genealogy, B. de Breffny (Cork, 1974)

British Isles Genealogical Register – 2000 (Federation of Family History Societies, CD-ROM, 2000)

The British Overseas: A Guide to Records of their Births, Baptisms, Marriages, Deaths and Burials, Available in the United Kingdom, G. Yeo (Guildhall Library, 3rd revised edn. 1994)

Catalogue of British Family Histories, T.R. Thomson (3rd edn. London, 1980)

Catholic Missions and Registers 1700–1880, M.J. Gandy (1993, 6 parts)

Census Copies and Indexes in the Library of the Society of Genealogists (Society of Genealogists, 3rd edn. 1995)

Census Returns 1841–1891 on Microform, J. Gibson (Federation of Family History Societies, 6th edn. 2002)

County Sources Guides (Society of Genealogists, London)

Criminal Ancestors: A Guide to Historical Criminal Records in England and Wales, D.T. Hawkings, (Sutton Publishing, 1996)

Current Publications by Member Societies (Federation of Family History Societies, 10th edn. 1999)

Current Publications by Member Societies on Microfiche (Federation of Family History Societies, CD-ROM, 5th edn. 2002)

Dictionary of Genealogical Sources in the Public Record Office, S. Colwell (1992)

The Dictionary of Genealogy, T. Fitzhugh (A. & C. Black, London, 5th edn. 1998)

Directories and Poll Books in the Library of the Society of Genealogists (Society of Genealogists, 6th edn. 1995)

Directory of Family Associations, E.P. Bentley (Baltimore, USA, 3rd edn. 1996)

Employing a Professional Researcher: A Practical Guide (Society of Genealogists, Leaflet 28, 1997)

Explore your Family's Past (Reader's Digest Association, 2000)

The Family Historian's Enquire Within, P. Saul (Federation of Family History Societies, 5th edn. with amendments 1997)

Family History Monthly, Diamond Publishing Group Ltd., Unit 101, 140 Wales Farm Road, London W3 6UG (Tel. 020 8752 8157)

Family History News & Digest, Federation of Family History Societies (Publications) Ltd., Units 15–16, Chesham Industrial Estate, Oram Street, Bury BL9 6EN

The Family Records Centre: A User's Guide, S. Colwell (National Archives, 2002)

Family Tree Magazine, ABM Publishing Ltd., 61 Great Whyte, Ramsey, Huntingdon, Cambridgeshire
PE17 1HL (Tel. 01487 814 050)

A Genealogical Guide, Major J.B. Whitmore (London, 1953)

Genealogical Research Directory (ed. K.A. Johnson & M.R. Sainty, Library of Australian History, Sydney, annual)

The Genealogist's Guide, G.B. Barrow (London & Chicago, 1977)

The Genealogist's Guide, Dr. G.W. Marshall (4th edn. 1903; reprinted London & Baltimore, 1967)

The Genealogist's Internet, P. Christian (The National Archives, 2nd edn. 2003)

Genealogists' Magazine, Society of Genealogists, 14 Charterhouse Buildings, Goswell Road, London EC1M 7BA (Tel. 020 7251 8799)

Genealogy for Librarians, R. Harvey (Library Association Publishing, London, 2nd edn. 1992)

The Good Web Guide: Genealogy (The Good Web Guide Ltd., 3rd edn. 2003)

Grantees of Arms before 1898 (Harleian Society, Vols. 66–68, London 1915–17)

Guide to Irish Parish Registers, B. Mitchell (Baltimore, 1988)

A Guide to the Post Office Archives, J. Farrugia (1987)

How to Use the Bernau Index (Society of Genealogists, 2000)

Irish Records: Sources for Family and Local History, J. Ryan (Flyleaf Press, Dublin, 3rd edn. 2003)

Land and Window Tax Assessments, J. Gibson, M. Medlycott & D. Mills (Federation of Family History Societies, 2nd edn. 1998)

List of Members, AGRA (£2.50 including postage)

A List of Parishes in Boyd's Marriage Index (Society of Genealogists, 6th edn. 1994)

Local Newspapers 1750–1920: A Select Location List, J. Gibson, B. Langston & B.W. Smith (Federation of Family History Societies, 2nd edn. 2002)

Making Use of the Census, S. Lumas (National Archives, 2002)

Maritime Sources in the Library of the Society of Genealogists (Society of Genealogists, 1997)

Marriage and Census Indexes for Family Historians, J. Gibson & E. Hampson, (Federation of Family History Societies, 8th edn. 2000)

Marriage Licences: Abstracts and Indexes in the Library of the Society of Genealogists (Society of Genealogists, 4th edn. 1991)

My Ancestor was a Merchant Seaman, C.T. & M.J. Watts (Society of Genealogists, 2002)

My Ancestor was a Policeman, A. Sherman (Society of Genealogists, 2000)

My Ancestors were Baptists, G.R. Breed (Society of Genealogists, 4th edn. 2002)

My Ancestors were Congregationalists, D.J.H. Clifford (Society of Genealogists, 2nd edn. 1997)

My Ancestors were English Presbyterians/Unitarians, A. Ruston (Society of Genealogists, 2001)

My Ancestors were Inghamites, P.J. Oates (Society of Genealogists, 2003)

My Ancestors were Jewish, A. Joseph (Society of Genealogists, 3rd edn. 2002)

My Ancestors were Methodists, W. Leary (Society of Genealogists, 2nd edn. 1999)

My Ancestors were Quakers, E.H. Milligan & M.J. Thomas (Society of Genealogists, 2nd edn. 1999)

New to Kew?, J. Cox (National Archives, 1997)

Nonconformist Registers of Wales, D. Ifans (National Library of Wales and Welsh County Archivists Group, 1994)

Oxford Companion to Local and Family History, D. Hey (Oxford University Press, 1996)

Parish Registers of Wales, C.J. Williams & J. Watts-Williams (Society of Genealogists, National Index of Parish Registers, Vol. 13, 1986)

The Phillimore Atlas and Index of Parish Registers, C.R. Humphery-Smith (Phillimore, 3rd edn. 2002)

Practical Family History, ABM Publishing Ltd., 61 Great Whyte, Ramsey, Huntingdon, Cambridgeshire PE17 1HL (Tel. 01487 814 050)

Probate Jurisdictions: Where to Look for Wills, J. Gibson & E. Churchill (Federation of Family History Societies, 5th edn. 2002)

Quarter Session Records for Family Historians, J. Gibson (Federation of Family History Societies, 4th edn. 1995)

Railway Ancestors: A Guide to the Staff Records of the Railway Companies of England and Wales 1822–1947, D.T. Hawkings (Public Record Office & Sutton Publishing, 1995)

Railway Records, C. Edwards (National Archives, 2001)

Record Repositories in Great Britain (Historical Manuscript Commission, 11th edn. 1999)

The Records of the Royal Air Force: How to Find the Few, E. Wilson (Federation of Family History Societies, 1991)

Records of the Royal Marines, G. Thomas (National Archives, 1994)

Register of One-Name Studies (GOONS, 14th edn. 2000)

School, University and College Registers and Histories in the Library of the Society of Genealogists (Society of Genealogists, 1996)

Scottish Family Histories, J.P.S. Ferguson (Edinburgh, 2nd edn. 1986)

Scottish Family History, M. Stuart (Edinburgh, 1930)

Sources for Anglo-Indian Genealogy in the Library of the Society of Genealogists (Society of Genealogists, 1990)

Specialist Indexes for Family Historians, J. Gibson & E Hampson (Federation of Family History Societies, 2nd edn. 2000)

Surname Periodicals: A World-Wide Listing of One-Name Genealogical Publications, I.J. Marker and K.E. Warth (GOONS, 1987)

Tracing your Ancestors in the Public Record Office, A. Bevan (National Archives, 6th edn. 2002)

Tracing Births, Deaths and Marriages at Sea, C.T. & M.J. Watts (Society of Genealogists, 2004)

Tracing your Family Tree, J. Cole & J. Titford (Countryside Books, Newbury, 1997)

Tracing your Irish Ancestors: The Complete Guide, J. Grenham (Gill and Macmillan, Dublin, 1999)

Tracing your Navy Ancestors, B. Pappalardo (National Archives, 2002)

Tracing your Scottish Ancestry, K.B. Cory (Polygon, Edinburgh, 2nd edn. 1997)

Using Libraries: Workshops for Family Historians, S. Raymond (Federation of Family History Societies, 2001)

Using Navy Records (Public Record Office Pocket Guide), B. Pappalardo, (National Archives, 2001)

Was your Grandfather a Railwayman?, T. Richards (Federation of Family History Societies, 3rd edn. 1995)

Welsh Family History: A Guide to Research, J. Rowlands et al (Federation of Family History Societies, 2nd edn. 1998)

Whitaker's Almanack, J. Whitaker (A. & C. Black, London, annual)

Will Indexes and Other Probate Material in the Library of the Society of Genealogists (Society of Genealogists, 1996)

Your Family Tree Magazine, Future Publishing Ltd., Beauford Court, 30 Monmouth Street, Bath BA1 2BW (Tel. 01225 442 244)

Research resources by period timeline

	Family records	State records	Church records
1800 to date	• Reminiscences • Family stories • Letters • School prizes • Newspapers/obituaries • Birthday books • Family Bibles • Internet surname lists • BIG R • GRD • *www.rootsweb.com* • *www.genuki.org.uk* • GOONS • What's been done before?	• *Family Records Centre, National Archives, Principal Probate Registry* • GRO Births, Marriages & Deaths • *www.freebmd.rootsweb.com* • *www.1837online.com* • *www.scotlandspeople.gov.uk* • Wills after 1858 • Censuses 1841–1901 • Commercial directories • Electoral rolls • WW1 records • Service records • Adoption • Divorce • Tithe maps • Poor Law Commissioners	• *County/Diocesan Record Offices* • *www.hmc.gov.archives* • Parish registers – christenings, marriages & burials • Bishops' Transcripts • *www.familysearch.org* • IGI, Marriage & Burial Indexes • Pallot, Boyd • *www.englishorigins.com* • National Burial Index • *www.familyhistoryonline.net* • Marriage licences, bonds & allegations • Clerical directories & clergy lists
1750–1800	• Research notes at SoG • Published genealogies	• Armed service records • Professions, trades & occupations • Nonconformists • IR/1Apprentices Tax • Estate duty registers • Poll books • University alumni • Assessed taxes • Bank of England Will abstracts	• Wills before 1858 • Inventories and administrations • Prerogative Court of Canterbury & local courts • Monumental inscriptions • Nonconformists • Quakers • Roman Catholics & Jews • Clergy induction papers
1660–1750	• Marriage settlements • Title deeds • Feet of Fines	• Annuities & Tontines • Association Oath Rolls • Oaths of Allegiance • Hearth tax	• Church Court records • Depositions, pleadings, morality, matrimonial, tithes, clergy, contested and disputed Wills, probate accounts • Communicant lists, Easter books
1538–1660	• Family muniments, • Estate records	• State Papers, Royalist Compounded Estates • Protestation Returns (House of Lords) • Lay Subsidies, Poll Tax	• Bishops Visitations • Glebe Terriers • Ecclesiastical licences • Midwives, surgeons, school masters, preachers • Parish registers/BTs
Pre-1538		• Inquisitions post mortem, Pipe Rolls	

County records	Parish/town records	Court records
• *County record offices* • www.a2a.pro.gov.uk • Poor Law Union records • Vaccination records • Bankruptcy • Maps, estate records • Business records • Coroner's records • Victoria County Histories • Tithe maps	• *County & borough archives* • Council minutes • Civic records • School records • Log books & admissions • Asylums & institutions • Municipal cemeteries	• *National Archives* • Criminal courts • Assize Circuits • Gaol Delivery • Criminal registers • Old Bailey Sessions • Court of Bankruptcy
• County Histories • Land tax • Militias & musters • Justices of the Peace & Quarter Sessions • Trades licences • Victuallers • Gamekeepers	• Parish chest • Churchwardens' accounts • Vestry minutes • Overseers accounts • Parish apprentices • Borough records • Guild & freemen records • Borough apprentices • Local charities • Hospital records	• *National Archives* • Courts of Equity • Chancery • Exchequer • Society of Genealogists – Bernau Index
• Justices of the Peace & Quarter Sessions • Poor Law examinations • Settlements • Bastardy • Removals • Hearth tax	• Settlement certificates • Poor relief	• *County record offices* • Manorial courts • Historical Manuscripts Commission – Manorial Register • Court Leet • Court Baron
• Maps • Local charters • Estate records	• Borough records • Society of Genealogists – Boyd's Inhabitants of London	• *College of Arms* • Court of Chivalry • Heraldic visitations
	• Town charter, markets	• Court of Augmentations

Index

AGRA (Association of Genealogists and Researchers in Archives)	41	family histories	11-13, 29
Ancestral File	30, 36	Family History Centres	36-7
ancestors	4-5	Family History Library & Catalogue	36
apprentices	29, 33	Family History News & Digest	34
arms	12-13	family history societies	33-4
army		Family Records Centre	14, 17, 18, 20-21, 26-7, 35
births, etc.	17		
personnel	35	FamilySearch	23, 30, 36
Association of Genealogists and Researchers in Archives (AGRA)	41	Family History Monthly Magazine	10
Australia	30	Family Tree Magazine	10
baptisms	21-6, 27, 30	Federation of Family History Societies (FFHS)	34
Baptists	26-7		
Bernau Index	30	FFHS (Federation of Family History Societies)	34
birthday books	4		
births	14-18	First World War	17, 35
Boyd's Marriage Index	23	forenames	16
British Isles Genealogical Register (BIG-R)	11	Genealogical Guide	12
		Genealogical Research Directory	11
burials	21-6	Genealogist's Guide	12
Catholics	26-7, 29	Genealogists' Magazine	12, 27
census returns	18-20, 31-2, 34	General Register Office	14-18, 30
Channel Islands census	18	GOONS (Guild of One-Name Studies)	13
charts	5-10		
civil registration	14-18	Grantees of Arms	13
clans	13-14	Guernsey	28
clergy	26, 36	Guild of One-Name Studies (GOONS)	13
coastguards	35		
college registers	29	IGI (International Genealogical Index)	23, 26-7
College of Arms	12-13		
Congregationalists	26-7	illegitimate births	16
county record offices	31-3	India	18
court records	34, 35	interests	11
dates	4-5	International Genealogical Index (IGI)	23, 26-7
deaths	14-18		
directories	28, 32, 33	International Reply Coupons	31, 40
Dr. William's Registry	26	Ireland	
East India records	18	census	20
electoral registers	32	clans	13-14
enclosure awards	33	family histories	12
Englishorigins.com	23, 27, 31	parish registers	26
Estate Duty Office	21	professionals	41
family associations	13-14	registration	17
family bibles	4-5	textbooks	10
family group sheets	6, 9-10	Will abstracts	28

Isle of Man	18, 27-8	printed	
Jews	27, 29, 30-1	books	33
Land Tax	32	pedigrees	12
Landed Gentry	29	professional searchers	14, 41
local studies libraries	31	professions	29
mailing lists	11	Public Record Office	
maps	28, 32	*see* National Archives	
Marine Register	17	Quakers	6-7
marines	35	railwaymen	35-6
marriage		Regimental Returns	17
certificates	16	Royal Air Force	35
parish registers	21-6	school registers	29, 33
licences	29	Scotland	
merchant seamen	35	Association of Family History	
Metropolitan Police	35	Societies	34
monumental inscriptions	28	census	20
Natal War Deaths	17	clans	13
National Archives	34-6	family histories	12
National Genealogical		Macleod Collection	28
Directory	11	parish registers	25
navy	35	professionals	41
New Zealand	30	registration	17, 28, 30
newspapers	28, 32	textbooks	10
nonconformists	26-7	Scotlink	17
non-registration	16	sea, events at	17, 23
Old Parochial Registers	25, 30	Social Security Death Index	36
one-name studies	13-14	Society of Genealogists	27-31
Ordnance Survey maps	32-3	solicitors	36
overseas	17-18, 20, 29-30, 36-7	South African War deaths	17
Pallot's Marriage Index	23	surnames	
parish registers	21-6, 28, 32	periodicals	11-12
passenger lists	29-30	variations	13
pedigree charts	6-10	textbooks	10
peerages	29	Times, The	30, 32
Phillimore Atlas	21	tithe maps	33
photographs	4-5, 10	tombstones	28
police	35	university registers	29
poll books	28	Wales	
Poor Law Unions	32	parish registers	25
postmen	36	textbooks	10
Prerogative Court of		Wesleyan Metropolitan	
Canterbury	21	Registry	26
Practical Family History		Wesleyans	26
Magazine	10	Wills	20-1, 28, 29, 30, 32, 35
Presbyterians	26-7	workhouses	32
Principal Probate Registry	30	World War deaths	17
Principal Registry of the		Your Family Tree Magazine	10
Family Division	20		

Notes